THE CRAZY WORLD OF

HOUSEWORK

CARTOONS BY

Bilsart

EXLEY
NEW YORK • WATFORD, UK

Other cartoon giftbooks in this series:
The Crazy World of Cats (Bill Stott)
The Crazy World of Football (Bill Stott)
The Crazy World of Gardening (Bill Stott)
The Crazy World of Golf (Mike Scott)
The Crazy World of Marriage (Bill Stott)
The Crazy World of Rugby (Bill Stott)
The Crazy World of Sex (Bill Stott)

First published in hardback in the USA in 1996 by Exley Giftbooks.
Published in Great Britain in 1996 by Exley Publications Ltd.

12 11 10 9 8 7 6 5 4 3 2 1

ISBN 1-85015-764-2

Printed in Singapore.

Exley Publications Ltd, 16 Chalk Hill, Watford, Herts, WD1 4BN, United Kingdom.
Exley Giftbooks, 232 Madison Avenue, Suite 1206, NY 10016, USA.

"I'm sorry to drag you out, Doctor – I'm worried sick about
him – he keeps tidying his room."

"Mom! Dad got the numbers on the washing machine wrong again."

"And when Cinderella had all the housework to do, did she say 'bloody' all the time like you?"

"O.K. Killer – what shall we do first – junior's bedroom?
The hall? The living room?"

"Have you seen my running shoes?"

"O.K. – the house is pristine. You have exactly 12 hours to wreck it."

"Dad? I think I just did a bad thing."

"Don't ask. My wife and I swapped jobs. She went to the office and I ran the house. She was so good they have made her manager and fired me."

"All I did was ask her if she'd like a new vacuum cleaner
for her birthday..."

"Hello Darling, I'm home. Good day?"

"Now, little man – has the nasty lady been cruel to you?"

"Definite smear, bottom left-hand corner..."

"Looks like you have an interesting evening
ahead of you, Clive..."

"Course – I've told your mother many times – with a little organization – housework would take about thirty minutes a day..."

"What a great shot! Quick, or you'll miss the replay!"

"Course – we saved a lot. Gerry fitted it – all by himself.
Didn't you Gerry?"

"If cleaning is <u>my</u> job – I do it <u>my</u> way – O.K.?"

"The lady on the T.V. smiles and laughs when she uses 'Glimshine' Mommy. Why aren't you smiling and laughing?"

"Mom! Mom! Sandy's thrown up in my toy box!"

"It <u>always</u> sucks the dog up on full power – don't you know anything?"

"Do your parents do this? The only time I <u>have</u> to tidy up is when the cleaning lady is coming!"

"Quick – more ketchup. They'll never guess how we did this!"

"And here on the home straight managing director, alias Mrs. Brownlow, needs a new lap record if she's going to make work on time..."

"Oh no, it's weird Mr. Weitz – you know, the 'new man' who actually <u>discusses</u> soap powder!"

"There's my little treasure – busy polishing the table
with fly spray."

"And while in the shower, you had a life and death struggle
with an enraged bull elephant did you?"

"So, the dog wrecked the kitchen floor?
In his own shoes, or yours?"

"A feather duster? You dust feathers? I didn't know we had any!"

"You got the cat 'Prettypaws'. She hates 'Prettypaws'."

"Mother says: 'Have you dusted this week?'."

"Hello Grandma! We knew you were coming because
Daddy tidied up."

"Will we share everything, when we're married? – Sure – housework – kids – everything – trust me..."

"Fair exchange? He decides what our stance is on nuclear disarmament, the Middle East and inflation and I do the cooking, decorating and shopping."

"Today – I thought – I'll be positive. Today I will organize myself. Today I will turn washing and ironing into an art form. Then I thought 'Stuff it' and had a glass of sherry."

"I wonder if we could all stand and move our chairs a little?
They make such horrid marks on the carpet."

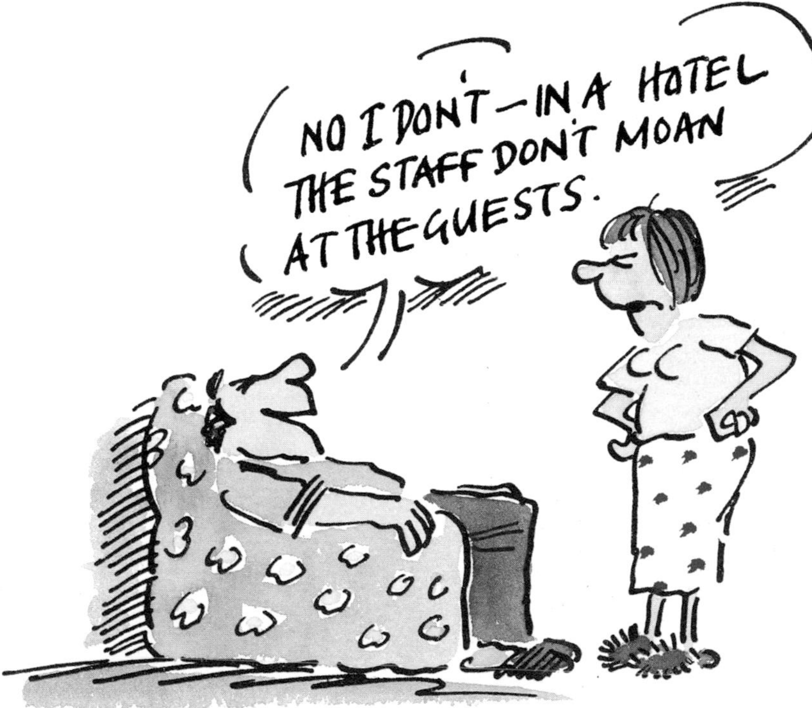
NO I DON'T – IN A HOTEL THE STAFF DON'T MOAN AT THE GUESTS.

"Dad! She's talking to the ironing again..."

"Me, obsessed with housework? Don't be silly!"

"The oven's bust, the vacuum's bunged up, my
three-year-old's got chickenpox – and you want to know how I
feel about double glazing? Clear off!"

"The shelf's up, Darling!"

"O.K. Let's just run through it again – 'Turbobrite' for the
bathroom, 'Wonderwood' for the furniture, 'Luvvarug' for
the carpets..."

"I tidied my room. Can I go out now?"

"Look Mummy, we're helping. We emptied the vacuum."

"I was a little tetchy at teatime after the oven blew up
just as the kids knocked over the tropical fish tank.
Sigmund Freud here wondered if I'd got PMS."

"Guess what! Today I washed the 5,798th sock
since we were married!"

"And while you were at the shops, the cat got in
the tumble dryer..."

"It's all right – poor soul's just realized you're off school
for the next six weeks…"

"My God! What happened? It looks like you had a baby
elephant through here!"

"Your mother's feeling better? That's good.
Yes, everything's fine here..."

"Dad! Mom murdered the vacuum cleaner!"

"My status! You can put me down as a presently inactive science graduate who's spent the last seven years raising kids, shopping, ironing, dusting and cooking."

"Would you like me to move?"

"We made you a cup of tea!"

"You don't mind tea in the hall do you?
The lounge carpet is new."

"Hmm – 'Imparts a brilliant shine on all domestic surfaces...'"

Books in the "Crazy World" series
($6.99 £3.99 hardback)

The Crazy World of Cats (Bill Stott)
The Crazy World of Football (Bill Stott)
The Crazy World of Gardening (Bill Stott)
The Crazy World of Golf (Mike Scott)
The Crazy World of Housework (Bill Stott)
The Crazy World of Marriage (Bill Stott)
The Crazy World of Rugby (Bill Stott)
The Crazy World of Sex (Bill Stott)

Books in the "Fanatic's" series
($6.99 £3.99 hardback, also available in a larger paperback format, $4.99, £2.99)

The Fanatic's Guides are perfect presents for
everyone with a hobby that has got out of hand.
Over fifty hilarious colour cartoons by Roland Fiddy.

The Fanatic's Guide to Cats
The Fanatic's Guide to Computers
The Fanatic's Guide to Dads
The Fanatic's Guide to D.I.Y.
The Fanatic's Guide to Golf
The Fanatic's Guide to Husbands
The Fanatic's Guide to Love
The Fanatic's Guide to Sex

Great Britain: Order these super books from
your local bookseller or from Exley Publications Ltd,
16 Chalk Hill, Watford, Herts WDI 4BN.
(Please send £1.30 to cover postage and packing
on 1 book, £2.60 on 2 or more books.)